BOOK
of TOASTS

Compiled by Patrice TenBroek

Book of Toasts
Patrice TenBroek

Published by Toasts Unlimited, LLC, Saint Louis, MO
Copyright ©2021 Patrice TenBroek
All rights reserved.

Project Management and Book Design: DavisCreative.com

Library of Congress Cataloging-in-Publication Data

Library of Congress Control Number: 2021917575

Patrice TenBroek

Book of Toasts

ISBN: 978-1-7378374-0-4

BISAC subject headings:
HUM015000 Anecdotes & Quotations
2021

From the Host
with the most
Toasts!

Here's to it and from
it and to it again and
if you don't do it
when you get to it you
may never get
to do it again.

May health hold
your hand and joy
fill your heart and of
the best days of
your life may this be
the start

Here's to the times we
may not remember and
the friends we'll
never forget

Here's to the land
we love and the love
we land

Here's to those that wish us well and all the rest can go to Hell!

May the hinges of
friendship never
rust, nor the wings
of love lose a
feather

May we be known
for our deeds and
not our mortgages

Here's to blue skies
and green lights

Here's to the health
of every friend
with joy and plenty
to the end

A Toast!
To many happy days,
rare good luck
and pleasant ways

It matters not if the
wine glass is half
empty or half full,
clearly there is room
for more

May you Lie, Cheat
& Steal
Lie with the one you
love, Cheat the Devil
and Steal away from
bad company

May every day bring
more happiness
than yesterday

Here's to us and
those like us...
Damned few
of us left

May all your
ups and downs be
under the covers

Laughter is the
shortest distance
between two people

A Toast!
To Love and laughter
and happily
ever after

May you have all the
health, wealth and
happiness in
the world

Love to One
Friendship to Many
Goodwill to All

Here's to your
health!
You make age
curious, time furious
and all of us envious

No road is long with
good company

To our best friends
who know the worst
about us but refuse
to believe it

As you slide down
the banister of Life,
may the splinters
never point the
wrong way

Here's Health to those I love and Wealth to those that love me

Here's to those who
have seen us at our
best and seen us at
our worst and can't
tell the difference

May the best of
happiness, honor
and fortune be
with you

To our absent
friends although
out of sight we
recognize them with
our glasses

To the Good Ole'
Days, which we are
having right now

Rejoice and be of
good cheer for
THEY are out there
and WE are in here

Let's drink to bread
for without bread
there would be
no toast

May you have all the
luck and happiness
that life can hold
and at the end of
your rainbows may
you find a pot
of gold

Here's to love,
the only fire
against which there
is no insurance

May you have hindsight to know where you've been, foresight to know where you're going, and insight to know when you've gone too far

Cheers to the
people who bring us
joy unintentionally with
their ridiculous choices
Idiots, we thank you

Blessed is the
season that engages
the whole world in a
conspiracy of Love

May you live forever
and that mine is the
last voice you hear

May your joys be as
deep as the ocean
and your
misfortunes
as light as the foam

May we live
to learn well and
learn to live well

To Life!
The first half is
ruined by our
parents and the
second half by
our children

Here's to
health, peace
and prosperity

Here's to those who
have seen us at our
best and seen us at
our worst and love
us anyway

May we look
forward with happiness
and backward
without regret

Its easy to be
pleasant when life
goes like a song, but
the person worthwhile
is the one with the smile
when everything goes
dead wrong

May your love ever
spread like jelly
on bread

There are good ships
and wood ships and
ships that sail the
sea, but the best
ships are friendships
and may they always be

Here's to staying
positive and testing
negative

May your home
always be too small
to hold all
your friends

May you live as long
as you like and have
all you like as long as
you live

Faith makes all
things possible, Love
makes all things easy
To Love!

Here's to health!
May we never be
without it

May the most you
wish for be the least
you get

May the warmth
of our affections
survive the frosts
of age

May friendship
propose the toast
and sincerity drink it

Here's to friends
and family who
know us well but
love us just the same

May good fortune
precede you,
love walk with you,
and good friends
follow you

May your life be like
good wine, tasty,
sharp and clear and
like good wine,
may it improve with
every passing year

I have mixed drinks
about feelings

At 20 we worry about what others think of us, at 40 we don't care what they think of us, at 60 we discover they haven't been thinking of us at all

Here's to a full purse,
a fresh bottle and a
beautiful face

Here's to Eternity!
May we spend it in
as good of company
as we find ourselves
tonight

Here's to good
friends,
Tonight is kind
of special

May neighbors
respect you,
Trouble neglect you,
angels protect you,
and heaven
accept you

May the best of
your yesterdays be
the worst of your
tomorrows

Over the lips,
past the gums,
look out stomach,
here it comes

Here's to
Raisin Toast!

To Toast!
Light with butter
and cinnamon

Pick a toast before dinner and as the evening progresses, look for the opportunity to work your toast in the conversation by claiming, "I have a toast for that!"

Toast with any beverage. Make sure glasses are filled. Click your glass gently to get everyone's attention. After the toast, touch glasses lightly with those sitting nearest you.

Moderately formal glassware makes it feel more like a celebratory occasion rather than a drinking game.

Toasting with a coffee cup or before noon is generally frowned upon.

After a toast has been delivered, each guest takes a sip. Knowing further toasts are likely to follow, don't drain your glass.

PLEASE DRINK RESPONSIBLY

WRITE YOUR OWN

WRITE YOUR OWN

WRITE YOUR OWN

WRITE YOUR OWN

Here's to staying positive and
testing negative

May the most you wish for
be the least you get

May your home always be too small
for all your friends

Here's to bread, for without bread there
would be no toast

ISBN 978-1-7378374-0-4

90000

9 781737 837404

True Love is like
a 4 leaf clover,
hard to find and
lucky to have

May we get what we
want and what we
need, but never
what we deserve

May you never
forget what is worth
remembering or
remember what is
best forgotten

_____

May you die in bed
at 95 shot by a
jealous spouse

May your troubles
be less and your
blessings be more
and nothing but
happiness walk thru
your door

May we be in
Heaven half an hour
before the devil
knows we're dead